THE CHRISTIAN SENSE OF HISTORY

Dom Prosper Guéranger

CALX MARIAE
PUBLISHING

IMPRIMI POTEST
Solesmes, 18 July 1945
Dom Germain Cozien
Abbot of Saint Peter's Abbey, Solesmes

IMPRIMATUR
Le Mans, 18 July 1945
HE Georges-François-Xavier-Marie Grente
Archbishop of Le Mans

Translated by Peter Mitchell and Peter Newman

The volume used for translation was published under the direction of Jacques and Rene Wittmann and printed on the presses of the *Protat Frères* publishing house, in Macon, 2 October 1945.

Copyright ©2022 Voice of the Family, Calx Mariae Publishing

Calx Mariae Publishing is an imprint of Voice of the Family, London, United Kingdom.

All rights reserved.
ISBN: 978-1-8384785-2-0

www.voiceofthefamily.com

CONTENTS

Preface		9
Chapter I	The supernatural in history	20
Chapter II	The action of holiness in history	34
Chapter III	The duties of the Christian historian	50
Chapter IV	Christ, the hero of history	60

PREFACE

The name and work of Dom Guéranger are too well-known for it to be necessary, at the outset, to introduce the restorer of *la vie bénédictine* to nineteenth century France at much length.

Prosper-Louis-Pascal Guéranger was born on 4 April 1805 in Sablé, a small village not far from the Priory of Solesmes, in the province of Maine. From an early age, he loved to make the monastery, desolated by the Revolution, the end of his walks, never tiring of admiring the statues which adorned the transept of its church. While still young, he showed a passion for study. His first readings of the works of the Jansenists and Gallicans made only a brief impression on him, while a tender piety towards the Word Incarnate and the Most Holy Virgin, towards the authority of Lamennais — at that time a defender of the papacy — and the recitation of the Roman Breviary quietly led him to his life's work.

After being ordained on 7 October 1827, he accompanied Msgr de la Myre-Mory, the retired Bishop of Le Mans, to Paris, in the capacity of secretary. Moments of leisure were not lacking and Fr Guéranger made the most of them; after two years, he published his first studies: *Considérations sur la liturgie*, *De la prière pour le roi* and *De la nomination des évêques*.

It was then that his desire for monastic life became clear. The Priory of Solesmes was up for sale; he resolved to purchase it and restore the Benedictine Rule, which had in the past produced so much fruit of learning and holiness. Providence blessed him with generous benefactors; some companions joined him, and on 11 July 1833, the new religious brothers moved definitively into the ancient house of the Maurists, where the Divine Office and the practice of the Rule would suffer no further interruptions, until the violent expulsions of religious orders from France.[1]

After four years of formation, work and suffering, the pope approved the Community's constitutions and established the priory as an abbey, to be the head of the Benedictine Congregation of France and heiress of the ancient congregations, and he raised Dom Guéranger to the dignity of abbot. Twelve days later, on the feast of Saint Anne, he made his profession at the Abbey of Saint Paul Outside-the-Walls in Rome, then returned to Solesmes. He celebrated his first Pontifical Office on the feast of All Saints, and prepared his religious brothers for their profession on the feast of the Presentation of Our Lady.

It is not necessary to detail every stage in the life of Dom Guéranger from this point until his death on 30 January 1875. The importance of his life lies less in the events which marked it than in the doctrine that he sowed. The governing of his abbey, living from day to day with barely sufficient funds, warding off threats to his work from politicians, legal experts and even from the clergy, founding new monasteries and responding to endless correspondence; all of this was not enough to fill his existence.

God had given this great monk a triple mission, which he would fulfil with zeal and courage, undismayed by the most terrible attacks. Whatever has been said of him, it

---

[1] The expulsion of religious orders from France would be initiated under the Third Republic from 1880-1901.

was not for love of conflict that the Abbot of Solesmes engaged in polemics during these years.. He would have much preferred the hard-earned peace of the cloister and the comfort of contemplation; he would have liked nothing better than to see other defenders of orthodoxy rise up to dispense him from having to intervene. He often waited, and, seeing no one else, he took up the pen to vindicate the truth. He would say later in life, "The good God put so much on my back! I did not interfere, however; it was He who charged me with it."

God charged him with restoring liturgical unity to the dioceses of France. The dioceses ignored him; each of them had their own special, recent liturgies. He undertook to introduce the Roman liturgy, which had captivated him since he first opened the Breviary and the Roman Missal. This was the goal of his *Considérations sur la liturgie catholique*, his *Institutions liturgiques* and, above all, his *Année liturgique*, which would allow the faithful "to regulate, in some way, their knowledge and contemplation of the mysteries of Christ and their practice of Christian virtues — through the movement and daily message of the Church's Liturgy". In less than twenty years, all of the dioceses of France had returned to the unity of the Roman rite — and God alone knows how his *Année liturgique*, "by its sweet and tranquil teaching, since 1841, has done good to the souls of those who, having tasted it, could not do without it — as if they recognised in it the voice of the Church and the sense of their baptism".[2]

God charged him to constantly defend Roman teaching and the prerogatives of the Apostolic See. The first

---

[2] Dom Delatte, *Dom Guéranger, abbé de Solesmes*, t. I, (1909), p. 294.

work from Solesmes was entitled *Origines de l'Église romaine*, which set out the succession of the first Roman pontiffs and a description of each of them, drawn from the historical sources available at the time. This was intended to remind an age of revolutions that there exists an authority which is forever sacred, a society whose role, surpassing all earthly concerns, is to render to God His elect; a centre out of which comes doctrine which enlightens, discipline which governs, and action which sanctifies. The lesson stuck, despite the ill humour of so many journalists, Gallicans and Jansenists.

In 1850, Dom Guéranger's love for the Church and for Our Lady prompted him to compose his *Mémoire sur l'Immaculée Conception*. Its vigour and insistence, animated by a profound and ardent faith, played a decisive role in the definition of the dogma which Pius IX would proclaim four years later. In 1870, when the pope convoked the bishops and the abbots for the Vatican Council, Dom Guéranger, who was unable to go to Rome, wrote his book, *De la monarchie pontificale*, for which the Holy Father immediately thanked him, saying that he had "rendered a real service to the Church" and "vindicated the rights of law, history, and faith, which have not been recognised". On 19 July, the bells of the abbey rang out for an hour, carrying into the distance the monks' faithful witness to the dogma of papal infallibility.

Finally, God would charge him to lead the fight against the great heresy of our times, naturalism, and to take up the defence of the supernatural. We must illustrate in a little more depth the role which Dom Guéranger played here, particularly in the field of history.

PREFACE

Towards the middle of the nineteenth century, Dom Guéranger witnessed with anxiety the return of impiety to France. Pernicious errors crept cunningly into the books of talented philosophers and historians, intending nothing short of the ruin of Catholicism. What was most serious was that an important group of Catholic writers and politicians sought more or less to enter into dialogue with evil. The liberal Catholic party, which was then organising itself, actually considered it astute to leave the field open to error and, instead of fighting it head on, to live in peace with it, in the hope of a reciprocal tolerance; which is, apart from anything else, impossible!

The error was manifested in all branches of human knowledge: theology, philosophy, history, literature. Taken as a whole, it formed the most subtle of heresies: naturalism, defined by the tendency to separate God from His creation everywhere, in order to affranchise man from His law.

Dom Guéranger's talent, learning, and faith prepared him better than anyone to unmask this evil. He tackled it wherever it appeared, but particularly in the field of history. A book entitled *L'Église et l'Empire romain au IVe siècle*, written by Prince A. de Broglie, the head of the liberal party, provided him with an opportunity. In a series of articles, published in *L'Univers* and later gathered into one volume, the Abbot of Solesmes showed the naturalism of his time in its true light. "The history of the Church," he wrote, "is so heavily influenced by Christian dogmatism that, if we do not take it into account, then it is impossible to write this history in a way that can be understood. Even if it were minutely exact as to the material facts, a history of the Church written by a historian who is not in all matters a disciple of the faith would not be completely true... The life of the Church is a divine act accomplished on the earth with the cooperation of man, and the Catholic alone holds the key to this mystery. Wanting to humanise this history is therefore a waste of time, and creating systems to explain it as useless as it is reckless."[3] And it is to this fanciful enterprise that the historians of this new school were dedicated.

After fifteen months of struggle, the publication of Fr Maret's book, *Philosophie et religion*, persuaded Guéranger to tackle naturalism in the field of philosophy. Without underestimating the merits of a few good chapters, he unhesitatingly condemned certain reductive doctrinal formulae, which had the effect of breaking the relationship between the work of Christian philosophy and its supernatural end. Such a condemnation succeeded in vindicating the just claims of the integral truth over the false principle of Christian philosophy as being not only distinct but separate from the faith. This philosophy, not content in distinguishing itself from other branches of human knowledge by its own methods and principles, went so far as to ignore (if not to exclude *a priori*) the existence of a superior truth and knowledge, in order to free itself radically and altogether from all the constraints of faith, even exterior and wholly negative.

Then came the episode which would give Msgr Pie, then Bishop of Poitiers, the material for his second synodal instruction. Dom Guéranger soon returned to his first subject and elaborated the definition of the duties of the Christian historian in four articles which we present here.

[3.] *L'Univers*, 8 March 1857.

PREFACE

The Abbot of Solesmes knew that the human mind is more curious about history than about philosophy; this is why, sensing greater danger from this direction, he went about his task with his characteristic ardour; saying of himself that "he was only a catechist who loved to explain the ABC of doctrine". In his turn, Dom Guéranger's biographer, Dom Delatte wrote:

> "Neither man, nor society, nor history can be explained outside of the Christian idea. If providence is not merely a word, if the Incarnation is not merely a myth, if the supernatural order is not merely a daydream, if eternity is not merely a mirage, then the vast ensemble of the life of humanity, which history presumes to present to minds, must have a meaning; a law; a direction. It cannot be that there is nothing but facts and dates — a pure spectacle — and that humanity, in the course of its long journey, has nothing to do and nothing to obtain."[4]

The reader will perhaps be surprised at the positions taken by Dom Guéranger and the assurance of some of his judgments. In our own day, we are no longer accustomed to search for a law in the history of the temporal and eternal destinies of men. Until recently, people would gladly say that they were sceptical on the subject of "so-called laws of history". Happily, they have drawn back from this dangerous scepticism. History is both an art and a science, and, as a science, its role is precisely to highlight the laws of life and death, belonging to the whole of human society.

[4.] Dom Delatte, *Dom Guéranger, abbé de Solesmes*, t. I, p.177.

One can, if one wishes, limit one's horizon to a strictly temporal point of view. But the believer prefers to ascend to great heights, where he can see further: he judges things and time *sub specie aeternitatis* ("in the light of eternity"). Where does man come from? Where is he going? Why must he live in society and submit himself to necessary authority which guarantees order; without which the freedom of all is unceasingly threatened? How does one distinguish authority from tyranny, order from constraint, and liberty from anarchy?

The philosopher and the sociologist answer these questions. But so does the historian — and in a manner which is perhaps more expressive — by the mere statement of the facts. He knows how to highlight the dominant role of morality and religion to the less informed. The Christian historian sees further and concludes with certainty: the morality of the Decalogue and the religion of Christ are the great explanation of history. People who violate the natural law go to their ruin, and the Catholic Church is the sole infallible guardian of this law. She explains it, develops it, and teaches it. She solves the enigma of evil; she shows man what ought to be his perfection, and she adds to the framework of history three essential parts that she alone knows how to recognise: she shows the first origin of history in the creation and the fall, its centre at Calvary and in the redemption, and its end in the last judgment. If this beginning and this end escape the grasp of science and erudition, at least the centre is there, where everything can be cross-referenced and verified. Here lies the key of history, its ultimate explanation; the essential fact that gives a direction to all the rest. The conversion of Constantine and the victory of the Milvian

Bridge, the deliverance of Orléans and the burning at the stake of Joan of Arc; these events appear — with their true, immense import — only to him who contemplates them from the height of Calvary. And it is he who truly knows the history of humanity.

This manner of writing history has produced masterpieces: such as the Apocalypse of Saint John, which proceeds by symbols, or the *Discourse on Universal History*, which Bossuet weaves out of raw facts. If this is sometimes forgotten in our own day then it is a misfortune, because we need to recognise the chaos in which we are in danger of perishing. We need to judge our time.

The words of Dom Guéranger can enlighten us on this point. Do not certain aspects of our own history make this desirable? Apart from certain works, written in a fanatical spirit, any short history of France, upon first contact with Joan of Arc, shows that there is a problem. The progress of historical criticism has, above all, in the last few years, brought to light how much remains to be learned and how much would have been gained by greater reserve in affirmations and denials. Moreover, the great catastrophes which are changing the course of things before our eyes, in a manner that great minds had not foreseen but that several wise men had guessed, give us considerable reason to revise our conclusions. Can we understand these facts? What great honour belongs to those who, long before this trial began, in the middle of the age of rationalism, defined a few historical facts around which all of history must be centred.

It seems that the nineteenth century itself takes the side of the Abbot of Solesmes, against all the doctors of naturalism who, for many years, blocked out his voice with their shouting. After all, few centuries were richer in supernatural testimonies: the thaumaturgic life of the holy Curé of Ars recalls those of the Desert Fathers; the holy shepherd girl of Massabielle, at the invitation of Our Lady, struck the source of the spring which continues to heal miraculously; Saint Thérèse of the Child Jesus, immediately following her death, caused the whole universe to confess that she is living still and continues to shower the roses of her charity on the world; and the Church herself, just when the world was denying her divine origin, solemnly defined her miraculous infallibility. It would take too long to describe here the magnificent contribution of modern France to Catholicism: France's contribution of thought, works, apostolic zeal and holiness, provoking the memorable words of Pius X: "If the supernatural lives anywhere here below, it lives above all in France!" And it is only right to recognise the fact that Dom Guéranger is one of the most vigorous instruments which God has made use of to defend and develop the reality of the supernatural at work in our country and in the world.

Moreover, Dom Guéranger demonstrates the truth of these principles by the fruitfulness of their application; courageously recalling them to his contemporaries in his writings on modern idolatry, on the abandonment of the practices of the Church, and on the apostasy of nations, which are true historical prophecies. For the rest, it suffices simply to look around today. Considered in the light of Christian doctrine, the history of our time becomes clear. Here, we recognise the combat of mysterious hidden forces: those of above and below clashing against each other. Our history resembles that which the author of the *Apocalypse* described nearly two thousand years ago, and it is not difficult to recognise the threats of the Beast; his lies, his blasphemies, his implacable tyranny, his colossal power of destruction; but this is far from upsetting us, for we know where the source of all hope and of all salvation is found: "God," says Bossuet, "has created a work in our midst which, detached from every other cause, holding to Him alone, fills all times and all places, and carries the character of His authority across all the earth, with the impression of His hand, which is Jesus Christ and His Church".[5] "Christ is at home in history," Dom Guéranger assures us in his turn; it develops under His reign; it moves towards a conclusion which will console us completely.

Happy the historian who sees these things and, describing them as he sees them, gives testimony to the King of the Ages!

Br Albert-M. Schmitt
Monk of Solesmes

[5.] Funeral oration of Princess Elisabeth Charlotte of the Palatinate.

CHAPTER I

The supernatural in history

In the same way that philosophy, for the Christian, does not exist as a separate discipline, neither is there, for him, any purely human history. Man has been divinely called to the supernatural state; this state is the end of man. The annals of humanity should offer a trace of this truth. God could have left man in his natural state, but it was pleasing to His bounty to call him to a superior order, by communicating Himself to him and calling him to the vision and possession of His own divine essence in his final state. Natural physiology and psychology are thus powerless to explain to man his destiny. In order to do so completely and exactly, one must have recourse to the revealed element; and all philosophy which pretends to determine the end of man by reason alone — apart from faith — is for that very reason tainted with and convicted of heterodoxy. God alone was able, through revelation, to teach man all that there is in the divine plan; there alone is the key to the real framework of man. Without doubt, reason can, in its speculations, analyse the phenomena of the spirit, soul, and body. However, for the same reason that it cannot grasp the phenomenon of grace, which transforms the spirit, soul and body, and unites them to God in an ineffable manner, neither can it fully explain to man what he is; either when sanctifying grace dwells within him, making him a divine being, or when this supernatural element has been driven away by sin, or even when, still unpenetrated by it, man finds that he has descended beneath himself.

Thus there is not, nor could there be, any true knowledge of man outside of the point of view of revelation. Supernatural revelation was not necessary in itself; man had no right to it; but God gave it and promulgated it, and thenceforth nature alone is not sufficient to explain man. Grace — the presence or absence of grace — enters into the first line of anthropological study. There is not one single faculty in us which does not call for its divine complement; grace aspires to cover man in all his depth, to fix itself in him in all its degrees; and it is so that nothing may be lacking to the natural and supernatural harmony in this privileged creature that the Man-God has instituted His sacraments, which take hold of man, lift him up and deify him — from the moment of birth up until the moment when he nears that eternal vision of the supreme good, which he already possesses but which he cannot yet perceive except by faith.

But if man cannot be known in his entirety outside the light of revelation, is it possible to imagine that human society, in its diverse phases called history, could ever be explicable without calling for that same divine torch which makes our nature and our individual destinies clear to us? Could *humanity* somehow have an end different to that of *men*? Will *humanity* be shown to be something other than *men* multiplied? No. In calling men to divine union, the Creator invites the whole of humanity at the same time. We will see this clearly on the last day, when all the millions of glorified individuals will form, at the right hand of the Sovereign Judge, that immense people that, as Saint John tells us, "no man could number" (Apocalypse 7:9). In the meantime, humanity (and I would like to say history) is the great theatre in which the importance of the supernatural element reveals itself in broad daylight; either through the docility of peoples to the faith, when it rules over the base and perverse tendencies, which make themselves felt in nations and individuals alike, or through misuse of human freedom, when it collapses and seems to disappear, which would result in the suicide of empires if God had not created them "healable" (Wisdom 1:14).

History must therefore be Christian, if it wants to be true, for Christianity is the complete truth; every historical framework that sets aside the supernatural order, in its exposition and appreciation of the facts, is a false framework: it does not explain anything and leaves the annals of humanity in chaos and in permanent contradiction to all the ideas that reason forms about the destinies of our race here below. It is because they have felt this, that the historians of our day, who do not belong to the Christian faith, have let themselves be led into such strange ideas when they have sought to provide what they call the "philosophy of history". This need for generalisation did not exist in the times of paganism. The historians of the gentiles had no "overview" of human history. The idea of homeland was everything to them; from the author's tone, one would never imagine that he was in the least bit caught up in any affection for the human species considered in itself. Moreover, it is only with the advent of Christianity that history begins to be treated in a comprehensive manner; Christianity, by always taking into account the supernatural destinies of the human race, has accustomed our spirit to see things beyond the narrow circle of a selfish nationalism. It is in the age of Jesus Christ that human fraternity has revealed itself, and only since then has general history become the object of study. Paganism, if it had ever been up to the task of writing a complete history of the world, would never have been able to write more than a cold statistical study of facts. It has not been sufficiently noted that the Christian religion created the true science of history by giving it the Bible for its base. No one can deny that today — despite the passage of the centuries, despite its gaps — we are all-in-all further advanced in our knowledge of ancient peoples than were the historians that antiquity itself handed down to us.

Thus, the non-Christian authors of the eighteenth and nineteenth centuries have borrowed the mode of generalisation from the Christian method, but have directed it against the orthodox system. They felt early on that, by taking hold of history and conforming it to their own ideas, they were dealing a harsh blow to the supernatural principle; so true is it that history testifies in favour of Christianity. Their success in this regard has been immense; not everyone is obliged to follow and appreciate a sophism, but everyone understands a fact — a series of facts — above all when the historian possesses that particular tone which each generation expects of those it privileges with captivating it. Three schools have taken turns in exploiting the field of history and, at times, they have done so simultaneously: 1) The fatalist school (one could say the atheistic), which sees only necessity in events and shows the human species grappling with invincible chains of brutal causes followed by inevitable effects. 2) The humanitarian school, which prostrates itself before the idol of the human race, proclaiming its progressive development with the help of revolutions, philosophies, and religions. This school quite freely consents to admit the action of God, at the beginning, as giving humanity its principle; *but*, once humanity is emancipated, God lets it go its own way, and it advances in the way of an undefined perfection, stripping itself along the way of everything that could be an obstacle to its free and independent progress. Finally, 3) the naturalist school: the most dangerous of the three, because it offers a semblance of Christianity in proclaiming on each page the action of divine providence. Its principle is to constantly minimise the supernatural element. For this school, revelation does not exist. Christianity is a happy and beneficial occurrence in which the action of providential causes appears. But who knows if tomorrow, if in a century or two, the infinite resources that God possesses for the government of the world will not bring about this or that still-more-perfect form, with the help of which the human race will be seen to run on, under the eye of God, to new destinies; and history will be illuminated with greater splendour?

Outside of these three schools, there remains only the Christian school. This school does not search about, it does not invent, it does not even hesitate. Its procedure is simple: it consists in judging humanity just as it judges the individual. Its philosophy of history is in its faith. It knows that the Son of God made Man is the king of this world — that "all power has been given to Him in heaven and on earth" (Matthew 28:18). The appearance of the Word Incarnate here below is, for this school, the culminating point of the annals of human history; this is why it divides history into two great sections: before Jesus Christ and after Jesus Christ. Before Jesus Christ — many centuries of waiting; after Jesus Christ — a length of which no man holds the secret, because no man knows the hour of the birth of the last of the elect, for this world is preserved only for the sake of those elect who will be the cause of the coming of the Son of God in His Flesh. With this certainty — certain with a divine certitude — history no longer holds any mysteries for the Christian. If he looks at the period which elapsed before the Incarnation of the Word, everything is explained before his eyes. The movement of the different races, the succession of empires: this is the way cleared for the coming of the Man-God and His envoys; the depravity, the darkness, the incredible calamities are the indication of humanity's need to see the One who is at once the Saviour and the Light of the world. Without doubt, God doomed this first period of man to ignorance and chastisement; yet far off, help was assured to him, and it was to this period that Abraham, the father of all believers to come, would belong; it is just, however, that the greatest effusion of grace should take place later, through the divine hands of the One without whom nothing can be just, either before or after His coming.

At last, He comes, and humanity, whose progress had been suspended, starts along the path of light and life. The Christian historian follows the destinies of human society even more closely in this second period, when all the promises are fulfilled. The teachings of the Man-God reveal with a supreme clarity the mode of appraisal which he must employ to judge events, their morality, and their significance. He has but one measure, whether he is dealing with a man or a people. Everything which expresses, maintains or propagates the supernatural element is socially useful and advantageous; everything which upsets, frustrates and annihilates it is socially disastrous. By this infallible procedure, he understands the role of men of action, of events, of crises, of transformations, of deteriorations; he knows in advance that God acts in His goodness, or permits in His justice, but never deviates from His eternal plan, which is to glorify His Son in His humanity.

But what always makes the eye of the Christian historian steadier and calmer is the assurance given to him by the Church, which marches unceasingly before him like a luminous column, divinely illuminating all his judgments. He knows what a close tie unites this Church to the Man-God, that by His promise she is safeguarded against all error in the teaching and general guidance of Christian society, that the Holy Ghost animates and guides her; it is in her therefore that the Christian historian seeks the rule for his judgments. The weaknesses of churchmen and passing abuses do not astonish him, for he knows that the goodman of the house has resolved to tolerate the cockle in his field until the harvest. If he must tell sad stories which bear witness to the passions of humanity then he is careful, at the same time, to attest to the might of God's arm, which sustains His work; yet he knows where leadership shows itself: the spirit of the Church, her divine instinct. He receives them, he accepts them, he confesses them courageously; he applies them in his narratives. Also, he never betrays, never compromises: he calls good what the Church judges to be good and evil what the Church judges to be evil. What does he care about the sarcasm and clamour of short-sighted cowards? He knows that he is in the truth since he is with the Church and the Church is with Christ. Others persist in seeing only the political side of events; they lower themselves to the pagan point of view: the Christian historian remains firm because he is certain in advance of not being mistaken. If, today, appearances seem to be against his judgment, he knows that tomorrow the facts, of which the import has not yet been revealed, will prove the Church — and him — right. This role is humble but what comparable safeguards do the fatalist, the humanitarian and the naturalist historians have? They put forward their personal judgment: everyone therefore has the right to turn their back on them. In order to get at the Christian historian, it is necessary to first demolish the Church on which he depends. It is true that, for nineteen centuries, tyrants and philosophers have been trying, but her walls are so solidly constructed that, until now, they have still not succeeded in detaching a single stone.

But if our historian, in following the sequence of the events of this world, sets out to research and report on the aspect which connects each one of them, more or less remotely, to the supernatural principle, then with even greater reason is he careful not to keep silent, not to conceal, not to mitigate extraordinary facts which God produces with the aim of authenticating and making still more palpable the marvellous character of the relations which he has established between Himself and humanity. First of all, there are the three great manifestations of divine power, which give, by means of miracles, the divine seal to the destinies of man on earth. The first of these facts is the existence and role of the Jewish people in the world. The historian cannot dispense himself from bringing into broad daylight the alliance that God first contracted with this tiny people, the incredible prodigies which sealed it, the hope of humanity that was placed in the blood of Abraham and David, the mission given to this feeble and disregarded race of preserving the knowledge of the true God and the principle of morality, in the midst of the successive defection of almost all peoples; the migrations of the people of Israel, first to Egypt, later to the centre of the Assyrian empire — as and when the theatre of human affairs displaced and scattered them — so that, on the eve of the day on which Rome, the momentary heiress of other empires, would find herself queen and mistress of the greater part of the civilised world, she would find that the Jews had preceded her everywhere. They were already there, with their oracles translated into the Greek language, known by all peoples; isolated, unassimilable, a sign of contradiction, but giving testimony that there would soon come — nearing day by day — He who must unite all the nations and "gather together in one the children of God, that were dispersed" (John 11:52).

It is with pleasure that our author will demonstrate this miraculous influence of the Jewish people, which defies all ordinary laws of history, by the prophecies entrusted to this people, which, for us, are not only the torch of the past, but which also preoccupied the gentiles so greatly during the centuries which preceded and followed the coming of the Son of God. Cicero had heard the echo of them when he spoke, with a sort of mysterious terror, about the new empire which was being prepared; Virgil, in the most harmonious of his songs, echoed the tone of Isaiah; Tacitus and Suetonius attested that the entire universe was turning in expectation towards Judah, with the general presentiment of seeing arise the men who were going to achieve the conquest of the world from that nation. *Rerum potirentur* ("They will take possession of all things"). After this, can it be denied that the study of history, in order to be authentic, must take on the tone and colours of the supernatural?

The second fact, which is tied to the first, is the conversion of the gentiles, both within the Roman empire as well as outside it. The Christian historian sets out to show that this immense outcome proceeds directly from the hand of God, who, in order to accomplish it, dispensed with simply providential laws. He points out, with Saint Augustine, the miracle of miracles; with Bossuet, the divine *coup d'état* which had its equal only at the moment when creation came forth from nothingness for the glory of its Author. He relates both the colossal grandeur of the goal and the insufficiency of the means; the significant preparations for so great a change, which presage that this world must belong to Jesus Christ, and, at the same time, that these preparations were in themselves just another obstacle to all human success in the venture; the Apostles, armed only with words and with the gift of miracles, which proved their authority and enabled them to win people over; the Jewish prophecies, studied, compared, and more deeply understood throughout the entire empire;

these elements becoming — as the writers of the first three centuries attest — one of the most powerful instruments of conversion; the superhuman constancy of the martyrs, whose almost incessant immolation, far from extirpating the new society, spread and affirmed it; finally, after three centuries, the Cross — the gibbet of the Son of Mary — crowning the diadem of the Caesars. Ideas, language, laws, mores; in a word, all things transformed according to the plan brought from Judea by this new kind of conqueror, whom the empire awaited and who knew how to triumph over it by shedding their blood under its sword.

The Christian historian is at ease amid of all these prodigies and nothing surprises him, for he knows and proclaims that everything here below is for the elect and that the elect are for Christ. Christ is at home in history; it is therefore quite clear that it cannot be explained without Him and that, with Him, it appears in all its clarity and grandeur. The next part of the annals of human history corresponds to the first; but ever since the publication of the gospel, the destinies of the world have taken on a new momentum; the earth, having waited for her King, now possesses Him. The supernatural preparation that was manifested in the role of the Jewish people, and that other preparation, at the same time natural and supernatural, that was manifested in the ever-progressive march of Roman power, have each reached their term. Everything is consummated; Jerusalem yields her rights and honours to Rome; Titus is the executor of the high works of the Heavenly Father avenging the blood of His Eternal Son. And yet the miracle of the Jewish people does not cease; it is transformed; and the nations will behold, until the eve of the last day, the spectacle, no longer of a privileged people, but of a people cursed by God. To the pagan empire, which, without knowing it, built the capital of the kingdom of Jesus Christ, God will give three more centuries to preside; thence will come the bloody edicts, which will have no other effect than to show the supernatural vigour of Christianity to future ages; then, when the time comes, it too will yield its place; from there it will go and take refuge on the Bosphorus, and the imperishable dynasty of the Vicars of Christ, which has not left its post since the martyrdom of Saint Peter, its first link, will wear the crown in the City of Seven Hills. The empire will crumble piece by piece under the blows of the barbarians; but before inflicting on it the humiliation and chastisement that its secular crimes have heaped on it, divine justice will wait until Christianity, victorious over its persecutions, has extended its branches high and far enough everywhere to tower over the waves of this new deluge; it will then be seen to cultivate, once again and with total success, the earth which has been renewed and rejuvenated by these waters, still more purifying than they are devastating.

Then, having presented all of these marvels, will the Christian historian change the tone of his accounts? Will he return to a simply providential explanation of the pomp of the earth? Are these marvellous things merely the central point of the annals of human history, such that henceforth the action of God must remain veiled under secondary causes until the end of time? God forbid!

A third supernatural fact, a fact which must last until the consummation of the ages, calls for his attention and requires all his eloquence. This fact is the preservation of the Church through time, without mixture in her doctrine, without alteration in her hierarchy, without suspension in her duration, without faltering in her march. A thousand great human affairs have begun, have developed, and have fallen into decline: the ordinary running of providence watched over them for the duration of their existence; today there is no more trace of them except in history. The Church is still standing; God sustains her directly; and every man of good faith, capable of applying the laws of analogy, can read, in the facts concerning her, this immortal promise that she bears at her base, written by the hand of God: she will last forever. Heresies, scandals, defections, conquests, revolutions: nothing has succeeded; pushed out of one country, she advances on another; always visible, always Catholic, always conquering and always under attack. This third fact, which is merely the consequence of the first two, ultimately gives the Christian historian the *raison d'être* of humanity. He concludes that the vocation of our race is obviously a supernatural one; that all the nations on earth not only belong to God, who created the first human family, but are also, as the Prophet said, the particular domain of the Man-God. And so, no more mysteries in the succession of the centuries; no more inexplicable vicissitudes; everything moves towards the goal; every problem resolves itself by this divine fact.

Admittedly, it takes courage to treat history in this mode today, above all when one is not of the clergy; when one believes sincerely, when one would not want for anything in the world to be full of the sense and manners of the fatalist and humanitarian schools. But the naturalist school is so great in number and talent, and so benevolent towards Christianity, that it is difficult to defy it completely and not to be, in their eyes, merely a mystic writer or, at most, a man of poetry, when one aspires to the reputation of science and philosophy. All that can be said is that history has been treated from this point of view by two great Christian geniuses and that their reputation was not thereby shipwrecked. The *City of God* by Saint Augustine and the *Discourse on Universal History* by Bossuet are two applications of this theory. The way therefore is masterfully marked out and, in following such men, one can endure the futile judgments of contemporary naturalism. Without doubt, it is no small thing to model one's intimate life on the supernatural principle; but it would be a grave inconsistency, a serious culpability, were this principle not to guide the pen. Let us look at humanity in its relations with Jesus Christ, its head; let us never isolate it, either in our judgments or in our narrative, and, when we consider a map of the world, let us remember above all that we have before our eyes the empire of the Man-God and of His Church.

CHAPTER II

The action of holiness in history

Can the Christian historian, once he is satisfied that he has broadly sketched out the supernatural character of the annals of human history, then believe himself dispensed from recording events of lesser importance, sown by divine power and goodness in the course of the ages in order to revive faith in successive generations? He will be wary of such ingratitude and, thrilled as he is to recognise that not in vain has the Redeemer of the world promised the visible signs of His intervention to His faithful until the end, he will be just as eager to initiate his brethren into the joy which he has experienced in encountering along his path a thousand rays of an unexpected light. Each one of these illuminations, though related more or less directly to the three great centres,[6] offers its own testimony of God's fidelity to His promises and a precious confirmation which springs forth embracing everything. Human history can thus contain miracles of detail, which can be seen to have had more than an individual significance and which have resonated through the ages. One need hardly add that, in

---

[6.] The divine governance of the Hebrews, the conversion of the gentiles and the preservation of the Church. (Cf. Chapter I)

order to enter into a serious and truly historical account, Christian historians must be certain from the point of view of impartial critique. Thus, the apparition of the Cross to Constantine has the right to figure seriously in the annals of the fourth century. As much can be said for the prodigies that were worked in Jerusalem during the same era, when Julian the Apostate wanted to rebuild the temple of Solomon. The miracles of Saint Martin, so influential in the extinction of idolatry among the Gauls, cannot be passed over in silence any more than those of Saint Philip Neri in Rome and of Saint Francis Xavier in the Indies, which, despite the blasphemies of the Reformation and the decadence of the papal Church in the sixteenth century, attested that she was nonetheless the unique heiress of the promises and sanctuary of the true faith. From the Christian point of view, would it not be leaving a gap in history to remain silent about the prodigious deeds that accompanied the introduction of the gospel to almost all the places where it has been preached? For example, the miracles of the monk, Saint Augustine of Canterbury, in his apostolate in England, and those which have been reported in the missions of the illustrious promoters of religious life, both in the East and the West, from Saint Anthony in the desert of Egypt to Saint Francis and Saint Dominic, among the other fathers of the thirteenth century? The chain of these marvels continues into our own time; it would thus be misunderstanding the role of the Christian historian to think that one had done enough by simply mentioning the deeds of this nature which occurred at the origin of Christianity. They have been constant, so to say, and they continue to be so; they are the pledge of the supernatural presence of God in the activity of humanity. Finally, they have had a real influence on peoples; one must thus take them into account if one judges them to be true; it is one's duty to record them and to assign them their role and their significance.

One hastens to add that not every form of history requires detailed research of supernatural facts; nor need ecclesiastical history be, strictly speaking, the only thing to which the Christian consecrates his talent for writing and recounting. Let this talent be exercised in all its forms, whether the history is general or specialised, whether it takes the form of memoirs or biography; all is well, provided that it is Christian, but the historian must expect to encounter the supernatural element early and often on his route; may he never then fail in his duty! If you want to write the history of France, nothing could be better, so long as you are up to the task; but just wait until you come up against Joan of Arc. Now, what will you make of this marvellous figure? You will not deny, nor describe ambiguously, facts which are now cleared up to the highest possible degree. Will you seek to explain them naturally? This would be a waste of time; there is nothing less explicable, from a natural point of view, than the mission and actions of the Maid of Orléans! Will you see in them the application of a providential law that governs human events, or the destiny of France in particular? But in them every sort of providential rule and ordinary law is inverted; we see nothing, either before or after, which leads us to think that God does such things in the general government of the world. Will you then say, in the academic style, that, all things considered, the mission of Joan of Arc remains inexplicable and that those who have wanted to explain it humanly have thrown themselves into difficulties that they could not get out of? Rather go all the way and frankly confess that history contains miracles and that the mission of Joan of Arc is one of them. Plainly admit that the shepherd girl of Domrémy truly saw saints and heard voices, that God clothed her with His invincible strength, that He put in her the spirit of prophecy, that He Himself made her victorious on the ramparts of Orléans, that He assisted her with the superhuman virtue of the martyrs in the sublime sacrifice which was to end this miraculous career. But then, note carefully the obvious significance of these marvellous facts. Who then is Joan of Arc? Is she simply a meteor with which God was pleased to dazzle us, with no other purpose than to show His power? Reason forbids us to think so and faith shows us, in this unequalled manifestation of divine predilection for France, the intention to save a very Christian kingdom from the yoke of heresy, which Protestant England would have laid heavily upon her a century later.

But Christian history does not limit itself merely to pointing out miraculous facts as clues of humanity's supernatural vocation; it is also important to study and point out the manifestations — at some times frequent, at other times rare — of sanctity throughout the centuries. God, in His counsels of justice and mercy, gives and takes away saints in different eras, so that, if we can speak thus, the "thermometer" of holiness is to be consulted if one wishes to judge the condition of a period or of a society. The saints are not only destined to feature on the calendar; they have an effect which is sometimes hidden, when it comes to intercession and expiation, but which is often apparent and efficacious long after their earthly life has ended. I am not speaking of the martyrs, to whom we owe the preservation of the faith, and one of the principal arguments on which our belief rests. The importance of their role in the history of the world is all too evident; but we cannot ignore the fact that at the end of the persecution of Diocletian, in the midst of the cataclysm of heresies which failed to submerge the barque of the Church in the fourth and fifth centuries, on the eve of the pagan-barbarian invasions, Christianity (and, thereby, society) was saved by the saints. Bishops, doctors, monks, consecrated virgins; what a list this age, which was like the second battlefield of the Church, offers us! Can the historian be silent in the presence of such an incomparable phenomenon?

Without doubt, he cannot dispense himself from citing an Athanasius, a Basil, an Ambrose, because these figures have, as they say, a historic role; but, however great these may be, they are far from representing everything produced by holiness during that period that had an effect in the visible order of the world. The role of Saint Augustine, for example, was not exactly "historic"; yet what man has had a greater influence on his age and on all those which have followed it? It would take too long to recount in detail how indebted the rest of Christendom is to these friends of God: Saint Gregory Nazianzen, Saint Hilary, Saint Martin, Saint John Chrysostom, Saint Jerome, Saint Cyril of Alexandria, Saint Leo. And let us not stop at seeing in them great geniuses and great men. Undoubtedly, great geniuses and great men of orthodoxy are a gift of God;

THE ACTION OF HOLINESS IN HISTORY

Bossuet and Fenelon in the seventeenth century are a gift of God; but when holiness is joined to genius, the action is something else entirely. The man of genius charms us; the saint enthrals us; we admire the great man, but the names alone of the saints — indeed, their very footsteps — move us: their memory makes us beat our breast, even after they have departed from this world.

Let us not believe that we have found the secret of the influence of the saints in the fourth and fifth centuries — to a greater or lesser extent — in the brilliant reputation that their knowledge and eloquence acquired for them, nor even in the rank which the majority of those whom I have mentioned occupied in the ecclesiastical order. The people revered a different grandeur in them: Valens trembled before Saint Basil, and Theodosius before Saint Ambrose, for a reason completely other than their "personal merit", to use today's language. It is God — God Himself — whom one feels in the saints; and this is why one is so powerless to resist them. Everyone knew that these men, who then formed the rampart of the Church, of which they were at the same time the light and glory, were of the same family as those heroes of the desert whose names and works were universally known; everyone knew that the majority of them had taken the habit before receiving the mitre. From West as from East, the faithful set out in droves to visit the deserts of Egypt and Syria, in order to contemplate and, if possible, to hear the Anthonies, the Pachomiuses, the Hilarions, the Macariuses; and, on returning to their villages, they rejoiced to find the sublime types of these men in the pastors charged with sanctifying them.

No, this cult of holiness, justified by so many examples, cannot be passed over in silence in the accounts of the age which followed the peace of the Church; it attests too clearly to the presence and action of the saints during these centuries, and thereby to the kind of supernatural assistance which God allotted to Christian society at that time.

The barbarian invasion, with all the misfortunes that accompanied it, would provide the historian with the opportunity to point out another role of holiness in the midst of these unprecedented disasters. The tumultuous hordes, rushing against the empire, encountered saints everywhere, and the saints were, to them, like a dike repelling the flood; holy bishops who stopped fierce chieftains in their course, holy pastors who saved their flock by giving themselves up to the sword; holy monks whose majestic simplicity disarmed the proud conquerors who had at first thought only of immolating them; holy virgins who, like Saint Geneviève, heartened cities and turned back God's scourges by their prayers. If one only studies the harsh period of the invasion in detail, one sees on all sides this astonishing phenomenon and becomes convinced that it is a point of historical truth to tell of these marvels and to admit that the only obstacle which drove back the barbarians — the only thing they respected — was holiness. Saint Augustine was lying on his deathbed in Hippo, when the Vandals came to besiege the city: they held off making the assault until the admirable bishop had rendered his soul to God.[7] It would be sad if

---

[7.] Recent historians, however, think that the Vandals did not make an assault, but discussed terms after a siege of fourteen months and that the inhabitants were saved (Gautier, *Genséric, roi des Vandales*).

the barbarians were shown to be superior to the Christians of our day in their appreciation of this heavenly element, which is never entirely lacking in the Church but which reveals its abundance to a greater or lesser extent, according to the needs of peoples and to whether justice or mercy is prevailing in the counsels of God.

The Christian historian can forget neither the works or the rule of the great Patriarch of western monasticism, to whom honour is given for having prepared the salvation of European Christianity, or that pleiad of holy bishops who shone in the sixth and seventh centuries, and who, by their councils and religious foundations, built, among other things, the kingdom of France "as bees make a hive", after the expression of Edward Gibbon. Let the historian not forget to state that the members of our monarchies, by their hundreds, are on our altars.

Nor will he omit to highlight the holy pontiffs of the Apostolic See, a Saint Gregory the Great, whose virtues ruled and governed both West and East with such meekness; a Saint Gregory II, the saviour of Italy; a Saint Zachary, the oracle of the Frankish nation; a Saint Nicholas I, doing so much, with such generosity, to snatch the Eastern empire from its ruin, by keeping it in union with the true faith. The historian will pursue those heroic apostles, dispatched by western monasticism towards the northern regions: not one of whom was not a saint; not a single one whose fruitful apostolate did not succeed through holiness.

But will the historian be able to pass over in silence that glorious phalanx of saintly emperors and kings, who, for three centuries and longer, appeared on the thrones and came to put a supernatural seal on the politics of the ages of faith? What a subject for study is the centuries-long influence on society of these crowned saints! A Saint Henry, a Saint Stephen of Hungary, a Saint Edward the Confessor, a Saint Ferdinand, and our own Saint Louis! And those saintly empresses, queens, duchesses: visible angels, the list of whom goes on further still, and who appeared in the midst of the peoples with whom they mingled in every manner, with the mission of cultivating and developing, by their sublime example, that Christian sense against which the corruption of nature protests ceaselessly and which ceaselessly needs to be revived! Can one think that it is enough to explain the active role of so many heroes and heroines of the throne by mentioning in passing that they were virtuous and that they have been counted among the number of the saints? No, it is necessary to delve further and to understand that here the point of view that is called *legend* is none other than the perspective provided by the most rigorous history. The benevolence of saintly kings and queens is one of God's principal manifestations in the supernatural leading of society.

When the historian finally finds himself facing the response of Christians in the eleventh century; a response which snatched Europe from barbarism; let him take care not to be mistaken. Let him attribute the triumph of the spirit over brute force neither to the genius of the former nor to the integrity of the latter; this would be contrary to all truth. This triumph was accomplished because God gave saints to His Church. If Pope Gregory VII had not been a saint, he would never have dared turn his mind to the task. What would Saint Anselm and Saint Peter Damian have done if they had been only pious pontiffs and knowledgeable doctors? In this century, Cluny was the fulcrum of the lever that moved the papacy, but let us not forget that it was built on four saints whose long lives covered one and a half centuries. How could one ever explain the action of Saint Bernard in the twelfth century without taking into account the radiant sanctity that shone forth from him? In the thirteenth century, who held up a society already teetering if not the seraphic Francis and the apostolic Dominic? Both, by their works and superhuman virtues, reawakened so powerfully the supernatural sense that was ready to fail. And in the university, what element, other than that of holiness, assured Saint Thomas Aquinas and Saint Bonaventure the supremacy which placed them so high above all the other scholastic doctors?

In the fourteenth century, Christendom seemed to collapse, fatigued by the rifts of the Western Schism, but still more so by the invasion of naturalism and sensualism, which the influence of holiness, in the thirteenth century, had been able to neutralise but not destroy. God then appeared more sparing with His saints. Apart from the illustrious Saint Catherine of Siena, we do not see a single saint whose action had any wide impact in this era. The historian will be sure to mention this aspect of the decadence which was just beginning to take hold; but he must also take care to study at leisure the sublime figure of Saint Catherine of Siena, in whom is summarised all the supernatural vitality of her time.

The fifteenth century, still more unfortunate than the one which preceded it, since it was the first to see anarchical doctrines formulated by the most celebrated doctors, and the standard soon raised against Christendom by the heresy of Wycliffe and Jan Hus — the fifteenth century, it must be said, was poor in saints. Its total did not come to half that of the thirteenth century. The extraordinary effect that Saint Vincent Ferrer produced on several kingdoms shows, however, that the sense of holiness lived on in the masses; but it must be added that this angel of God's judgment had already ended his career in 1419.

Then came the sixteenth century, a time of terrible trials in its first half; an era of triumph in the second. The historian will be sure to demonstrate from the facts that saintliness showed itself in an analogous proportion. Saint Cajetan almost filled the first half by himself; but barely had the year 1550 begun when a marvellous flowering appeared on the branches of the secular tree of Christendom, and, while Protestantism had at last stopped its conquests, it pleased God to show that the Roman Church had lost nothing, since she kept the gift of sanctity. A Christian history of the sixteenth century would have to be done again if it did not appreciate the restoration of Christian morals prepared by Saint Cajetan and continued with such vigour and magnitude by Saint Ignatius of Loyola and the saints of his Society, the reform of discipline formulated in the wise decrees of the Council of Trent and implemented by popes like Saint Pius V and bishops like Saint Charles Borromeo; the apostolate of the gentiles reborn in Saint Francis Xavier, that of Christian cities in Saint Philip Neri; the cloister purified through Saint Teresa, Saint John of the Cross, and Saint Peter of Alcantara. One must go back to the fourth century if one wishes to see such a radiant constellation of saints as that which shone in the firmament of the Church when the pretended reform had finally determined its borders. But among all those glorious names, France furnished only one saint: the historian will have to account for such a peculiarity.

The seventeenth century came, and although it had a lesser halo of sanctity than the preceding century, it still offered some particularly beautiful manifestations of the supernatural principle among men of God. Saint Francis de Sales deserves to command the attention of the historian for quite some time. In him the Catholic Church was, so to speak, incarnate; by his inviolable faith, his boundless charity, and his unceasing struggle; the holiness of Saint Francis overflowed in the writings which revived and regulated piety in all Catholic nations, but especially in France. James I of England said to his Anglican bishops, showing them a copy of the *Introduction to the Devout Life*, "Make us some books like that." This heretical prince had at that moment a sense of holiness; the sense that is recommended to the Christian historian. Any history is not complete if it is not, at the same time, a literary history to a certain degree. Our historian is advised not to omit the writings of the saints. Above all, let him not confuse them with ingenious inspirations and labours of piety. Pages written by saints have a particular savour which cannot be attained unless one is holy; it is known from experience that Saint Teresa, for example, moves the reader in quite a different way to that of the most vaunted spiritual writings of the seventeenth century.

France owes a great deal to Saint Francis de Sales, and it is right to regard him as one of the principal authors of the ascent of the Christian sense with which our own nation was favoured for half a century. Thanks to its response to the work of Saint Francis de Sales, France during this period could once again be counted among the nations in which saintliness flourished. It gave Christendom Saint Peter Fourrier, Saint John Francis Regis, Saint Jane Frances de Chantal, Saint Vincent de Paul; but these heroes complete the list of French saints in the seventeenth century. It ends in 1660 and, after that, France, glorious in so many ways, remained sterile in saints.[8] Although it is precisely this period which is most celebrated today, the historian should not fail to look into the causes of this disturbance of the Christian sense among us, in the very same era that people wrote with such eloquence on religious subjects. Perhaps he will be able to explain how, starting from the Régence in 1715, France was exploited, with great success, by a spirit of unbelief which nothing could stop. Evidently the supernatural sense was impoverished; naturalism had quietly gained ground. There were still two servants of God, however, who, having shone in the last years of the seventeenth century, continued their careers into the eighteenth: Saint Jean-Baptiste de la Salle and Saint Louis de Montfort; but it must be added that they were unrecognised, persecuted, and censured; and that, if God had not kept watch over the gift which he had given us in them, their reputation and their works would have died

---

[8.] The end of the 17th century saw the illustrious Sister of the Visitation, Saint Margaret-Mary Alacoque, who is at the origin of the modern devotion to the Sacred Heart. But, at the time of the essay being written in 1858, her process of canonisation was far from complete.

in contempt and oblivion. Besides, let one read the books written to revive Christian piety in the second half of the seventeenth century and see if there is frequent mention of the marvels of holiness bursting forth outside of France during this period. Did our fathers find, among authors of renown, any allusions to Saint Mary Magdalene de Pazzi or Saint Rose of Lima, who filled this same century with the perfume of their virtues and whose names were such common knowledge everywhere else? Can one conceive that the prodigies and even the name of Saint Joseph of Cupertino, known throughout the Catholic universe, took so long to cross the Alps? That a Duke of Brunswick, who was witness to the divine marvels manifested in this servant of God, abjured his Lutheranism in front of him for this reason, thus renouncing forever the rights of his sovereignty? Or that the marvellous instrument of this famous conversion, this personification of the holiness of the Church, living a few hundred leagues from Paris, was not invoked against the Huguenots, either before or after the Edict of Nantes? But all channels of communication were closed on this side. In the fifth century, Saint Simon Stylite, from the depths of the East and from the top of his pillar, recommended himself to the prayers of Saint Geneviève in Paris; in the seventeenth century, however, a miracle worker, who surpassed most of the saints in marvels, could live and die in a neighbouring country without anyone in France, other than the religious of his order, having taken the least notice of him! Can we therefore be surprised by the blasphemies and imbecilic laughter that were provoked by the publication of the life of Saint Joseph of Cupertino? It bears repeating: our historian, if he wants to deepen Christian morals, as he ought to do, must concern himself with these strange phenomena.

The eighteenth century, in its turn, will reveal to him, through its most marked diminution in the number of saints, a general symptom of the weakening of Christian society. Never was the "thermometer" of holiness (an image to which we have already referred) more exactly applicable. The century of naturalism did not deserve God hurrying to make a display of the supernatural. Some marvels, however, continued to burst forth at the heart of the Church, where life can never die out. Saint Veronica Giuliani, decorated with the stigmata of Christ's Passion, was one of a great number of saints: Saint Leonard of Port-Maurice, Saint Paul of the Cross, Saint Alphonsus de Liguori; each one of these saints, through their daily practice of heroic virtues, merited the honour reserved to them of being raised to the altars. France, however, could no longer present to the world anyone from among her children who appeared to be destined for such honours, until — from the bosom of the most corrupt court which our history has ever seen — two women in succession, both related to Saint Louis, seized the palm of sanctity which the Church, we hope, will confirm sooner or later. The first, a virgin and disciple of Saint Teresa, was Louise-Marie of France;[9] the other, a wife and queen, was Clotilde of Sardinia.[10] These two princesses — and a beggar, Benedict Joseph Labre[11] — are the only manifestations of holiness which France seems to have produced in the whole

---

[9.] Declared Venerable by Pius IX.
[10.] Declared Venerable by Pius VII.
[11.] Canonised by Leo XIII.

course of the eighteenth century and, when they appeared, the nation was on the eve of being handed over to the enemies of the supernatural order, who would have reduced it to a heap of bloody ruins, if God's merciful hand, which wanted to chastise and instruct us, but not to annihilate us, had not finally broken the oppressors of His people.[12]

This somewhat incomplete enumeration of the resources which the study of holiness in each century offers to the Christian historian, has taken too long; it can be summarised in a word: if the historian possesses the gift of faith, he will ensure he makes use of it in his accounts of significant supernatural events in the history of nations, for such events are the continuation and the application of the three great miracles on which the entire history of humanity revolves.[13]

If he wants to describe and portray the morals of Christian peoples, let him gauge the measure of holiness in each century; let him show that it is through the influence of holiness that the faith is sustained and morality preserved; in a word, let him give high priority to the saints in his writings, if he wants to pen a history such as God sees and judges it.

---

[12] At the time of Dom Guéranger, there was not yet any discussion of the beatification of the Martyrs of the Revolution. Though we may consider them as having already made up a part of the magnificent phalanx of the saints of the 19th century, Dom Guéranger's judgment of the end of the 17th century and the 18th century is, by and large, to be retained.

[13] See footnote 6.

CHAPTER III

The duties of the Christian historian

Let us add some more detail to the principles formulated above by saying something about the tone of the historian and his judgments. Everyone can see, with a bit of reading, that nothing differs more from the Christian tone than the philosophical tone, and the reason for this is simple: it is that there is no-one more dissimilar to a Christian than a philosopher. There is no need to give a long definition of the sort of philosopher that is meant here. It is the one who, having been baptised and living in the heart of a Christian society, systematically makes abstractions in his language of the ideas suggested by the faith of the Church, in which he has been raised, and who speaks as if his thought no longer had anything in common with the supernatural order. A book written in the tone of a philosopher, when its author is a Catholic, is always a scandal; this is easily understood as soon as one reflects that nothing is more dangerous for man than to favour in himself the rationalist tendency. Faith is a virtue; not the result of scientific labour; it is often menaced by the enemy of mankind who, with good reason, sees in faith the means by which our intelligence is enlightened with the light of God Himself. This is also why the Christian not only has the duty to *believe* but also to *confess* what he *believes*. This double obligation, based on the doctrine of the Apostle (Romans 10:10), is even more incumbent in the age of naturalism, and the Christian historian must understand that it is not enough to declare his belief in this or that passage of his book, if the Christian tone then disappears to make way for the philosophical tone. At first, some will doubt him, and this is already a misfortune; others, more numerous, taking no account of his profession of faith, will fortify their naturalism from the parts of his book where he writes like a philosopher; and, to repeat, this is a real scandal. What good is a book, written entirely by a believer, in which the reader never detects the Christian tone? There are some, however, for whom such an amazing feat is an act of impartiality, at least to their way of thinking. As if the Christian were permitted to be impartial as regards the faith and its applications! Let the tone of the believing historian always be a Christian tone, and may the reader constantly recognise, in the style of a child of the Church, the fullness and firmness of the doctrines which are in him.

Historical judgments have a singular importance, above all when the historian is regarded favourably. These judgements are sometimes formulated with a certain authority or, at other times, result from the arrangement of historical accounts and the choice of terms used; both are things that the reader particularly looks for in a work of history. When I speak of historical judgments, I am not speaking of facts: for the latter, there is only the truth, and the Christian historian must be above all a truthful narrator. He must not flatter anyone, nor disguise anyone's wrongdoings; at the same time, he must not be afraid to do justice to the thousand calumnies which have made history one immense conspiracy against the truth. Thus, he will keep the right balance and show himself faithful, demonstrating the most rigorous impartiality. So much for the facts. As for his judgments and appraisals, it is evident that the Christian must differ completely from the philosopher. For it to be otherwise would be quite simply absurd, and a lack of conviction in such a matter would be gravely reprehensible. A Christian judges facts, men, and institutions from the point of view of the Church; he is not free to judge otherwise, and that is his strength. A Christian historian whose judgments are accepted by philosophers is unfaithful, or else the philosophers in question are no longer philosophers. It is therefore necessary to be resolved to shake things up, or, if one does not have the courage for this, to abstain from writing history. There are enough of these hybrid books whose believing authors, by their judgments, are in chorus with those who do not believe. It is these innumerable betrayals which have given birth to so many prejudices and to just as many inconsistencies; an invincible obstacle to the formation of a strong and solid Catholicity.

But, say some writers, skilful at disguising their faith under a fashionable verbosity, always ardent to extol what they call the ideas of modern society: *do you want us to write history in the tone of a devotional work? Should we therefore write our books, our articles, as if they were sermons, as if they were treatises of theology or canon law?* No. Each thing has and ought to have the tone that is proper to it; but history is the great theatre where the supernatural performs, and you must have the courage to present it to your readers. You speak to us with admiration of the *City of God*, of the *Discourse on Universal History*; you say: *now that is the Christian genre of history!* But what, pray, does your own manner have in common with that of Saint Augustine or Bossuet? They tell all, they judge all from the point of view of Jesus Christ and His Church; they do not write an ascetic work because it is not appropriate; but, on the other hand, they set out to show, not only in the whole but right down to the details, how the supernatural principle governs and explains everything; at every line, one senses that they are Christians and, in reading them, one becomes more Christian oneself. Such is the historian when he is inspired by his faith.

You hesitate to proclaim the most obvious miracles, you seek explanations for them which play down their extraordinary nature, at the risk of weakening the faith of your readers; you leave out prophecies, you conceal sanctity and its action, in order to place men, albeit great men, centre-stage; while confessing the divinity of the Church, you insist above all on making it look just like human society; in a word, you do not deny the supernatural, but you put it in the dock for fear of frightening away your audience and so as to appear a *man of your time*. Saint Augustine and Bossuet did quite the opposite. A philosopher, M. Saisset, has given us a translation of the *City of God*; in the preface, while expressing his admiration for the Bishop of Hippo, he regrets that this great genius too often stops to make childish interpretations of the Bible and to recount miracles — overly reminiscent of a Christian priest. Could today's historians ever merit such a reproach? This would be the sign that one had written as one ought to when one is enlightened with the light of faith. Indeed, Saint Augustine pauses frequently, and at length, on prophetic oracles, and he illuminates his stories with an exegesis as scholarly as it is mystical; but is the principal means of understanding Christianity not to seek this understanding from the prophetic events from which it is derived? Saint Augustine develops, in immortal language, the argument which emerges from the miraculous propagation of the gospel and, at the same time, he stops to recount the prodigies worked in Africa, before his own eyes and the eyes of his people, by the relics of Saint Stephen. Some of our Catholics, affected by naturalism, wonder why such a great genius spoils such a great subject with anecdotes of such little import. They get lost in their regret that such details make him lose sight of the overall idea! It is they, alas, who have lost sight of the overall idea! They do not see the significance of these miraculous episodes, contemporary to the great doctor. They do not understand that, after he has demonstrated the divinity of Christianity by the fact of its propagation, brought about contrary to all laws of history and all conditions of human nature, it still needs to be proven that the Catholic society to which he belongs, of which he is a bishop, is in fact that Christianity which God alone has established by the irresistible strength of His arm. And it is through the permanent gift of miracles that this identity is proven, and this is why Saint Augustine does not think he is derogating from the vast plan of the *City of God* when he descends into apparently minor facts, of which he has been a witness, and in support of which he can invoke the testimony of his people. These are precious considerations for the Christian historian, and an eloquent confirmation of the principles which we have laid out in the preceding chapter.

One must not fear therefore, when writing history, to incur the reproach of a certain mysticism, if one understands by this the supernatural tint of an account where the marvellous action of God is revealed at each step. Let us beware of blushing for this reason; there are enough people who have set out to expel God and His Christ from history for there to be some distinction in bringing Him back. But I have yet to respond to another bias, owing to the imprudent concessions which certain historians have believed they could make to naturalism. They persuade themselves that these indulgences are a means of attracting the faith of philosophers, by revealing a sort of analogy to them; a sort of fraternity, between the Christian and philosophical viewpoints. Thence these phrases of rationalist origin; these watchwords by which they hope to make themselves heard. There are two drawbacks to this. The first, which is not the least grave, is that your histories and articles, falling under the eyes of weak Catholics, for whom they are not intended, only serve to diminish the ardour of their faith and to plunge them even further into the current crisis from which they urgently need to escape. It would be helpful for them to come upon books apt to nourish their belief; they read you with confidence, because they know that you are Catholic like them, and this reading leaves them in a worse state than before. The other drawback is that, far from bringing back the philosophers to the faith, you increase their pride. They triumph to see Catholics at their tail; they applaud their own progress, having succeeded even in imposing their language and ideas. They only notice the awkwardness of your position because you are reduced to pursuing two aims simultaneously: firstly, your belief, which you hold to above all, and, secondly, the demands of what you call the spirit of modern society, to which you do not want to show any infidelity either. These opposites merge as far as they can in your work; but be assured that, while you inevitably scandalise some of your brethren, you will not succeed in bringing back the others.

Let it be well understood, today more than ever, that society needs doctrines that are strong and consistent. In the midst of the general dissolution of ideas, assertion alone — assertion which is firm, nourished, without alloy — can make itself accepted. Debates are becoming more and more sterile, and each of them chips away a piece of the truth. As in the first days of Christianity, it is necessary for Christians to shock everyone by the unity of their principles and judgments. They have nothing to learn from this chaos of negations, and experiments of every sort, which attest so strongly to the powerlessness of contemporary society. This society no longer lives, except in the scattered debris of ancient Christian civilisation that revolutions have not yet taken away and that the mercy of God has preserved from shipwreck until now. Show yourself, therefore, as you really are: a convinced Catholic. Society, perhaps, will be afraid of you for a while; but be sure, it will come back to you. If you flatter it by speaking its language, you will amuse it for an instant, and then it will forget you; for you have not made a serious impression on it. It will recognise itself in you to a greater or lesser extent and, as it has little confidence in itself, it will have no more confidence in you.

There is a grace attached to the full confession of the faith. This confession, the Apostle tells us, is the salvation of those who make it, and experience shows that it is also the salvation of those who hear it. Let us be Catholics, and nothing but Catholics; not philosophers or utopian dreamers, and we will be the leaven by which Our Lord will ferment the whole dough. To repeat, it was just so at the beginning. If society has a chance of salvation, it is through the more and more resolute attitude of Christians. Let it be known that we do not compromise on anything, that we disdain to repeat the jargon of philosophers. It is a point of fact that Christianity imposes itself, not by violence, but by virtue of the conviction that it preaches.

Besides, each time a demonstration of this frankness is given, it never fails to excite sympathy. When M. de Montalembert published the *Life of Saint Elizabeth*, there was indeed some astonishment; some murmurs about the *Introduction*, in which the Catholic sense expressed itself with such freshness. It would be difficult to fly in the face of historical naturalism with more energy than the author had done. Did the *Introduction* and the work which followed it suffer for that? Its numerous editions are there to attest in the negative. And yet, it would be necessary to go back two centuries to encounter a book written with such Catholic cheek. Here was the germ of a whole revolution, and the example profited others. But its influence has not extended as far, nor as wide, as was to be desired. Too often since then we have had Catholic historians who, contrary to the counsel of the Saviour, have wished to sew pieces of worldly wisdom (which, though rejuvenated, are always old) onto the ever-new garment of the Christian faith. Where does this illusion come from? Should one see in it a mark of the abasement of character which the same authors point out with such insistence? One dares not say it, for this would be to turn against them, no doubt unjustly, the very reproach that they address to others. But one may be permitted to think that, if the sense of Christian dignity was made clearer to them, they would be less ready to offer incense to modern prejudices; that, like Donoso Cortés, they would finally notice that, for many years already, we have had our backs turned to progress; that the wheels of our chariot are buried up to the hub in a rut, in which we will perish unless we get ourselves out by a supreme effort. To imagine oneself acting in the faith and, at the same time, in naturalism is just as unreasonable as wishing to act simultaneously according to a policy of order and disorder. Everything that one attempts with this method turns to evil, and the conquests that one makes in this way are not conquests at all; the wonderful success of managing to agree on the use of certain words, as perfidious as they are sonorous, while an abyss separates the parties as to the sense that these words represent! These ideas need reforming, for which I know of nothing more effective than to tell history, once and for all, just as it is; with all its supernatural instructions, which make the figure of Christ soar above the greatest, as well as over the smallest movements of humanity.

The ultimate misfortune of the Christian historian would be to take the ideas of today as a rule of assessment and to carry them into his judgments on the past. On the contrary, he needs to see them for what they are: hostile to the supernatural principle. He needs to take stock of the ravages of modern paganism and, in order not to succumb, he must have his eyes fixed unceasingly on the immutable revealed truth, which manifests itself in the teaching and practice of the Church. "A sense which is the enemy of the faith, an overexcitement of the pagan spirit," says M. de Champagny, "was the wind that drove the tempest of 1789." If you still stand in admiration of the *conquests* of those days, I fear greatly for your historical judgments and for the tone of your accounts, whatever your intentions of orthodoxy might be. Blessed the historian who, amid the *mêlée* of contradictory principles, free of all desire for popularity; a disciple, even in the smallest things, of that Church to which belong time and eternity to come; blessed the historian who knows how to pass through such a terrible crisis without sacrificing the smallest truth along the way!

CHAPTER IV

Christ, the hero of history

As important as it is to protect Catholics from naturalist tendencies in the judgment of historical facts, it is just as necessary, and with far greater reason, to inform them that this naturalism does not exist simply at the level of theory; that, for a long time, it has been generally insinuated and even applied in the majority of the writings which have been published, even by authors with orthodox intentions, on historical questions, whether general or specialised. Nothing is rarer than history books in which the Christian sense is never lacking. The historian who, in his private language and in his practice, is a faithful disciple of the Church, takes up the pen, only to indulge in verbose philosophising in relating and explaining the facts. This double language (this double life) is a misfortune; but furthermore, it is a danger for readers, above all for young people. As a consequence few of these Christian readers and young people are left with their integrity intact as it used to be, and how it is to be wished that this was not the case!

It is not my intention here to make a review of universal history, nor to identify the thousand points at which a way has been found for naturalism to infiltrate; I will limit myself to showing, in passing, some traits which serve as an illustration. In general terms, naturalism can be identified in a book when the author seeks to veil the action of God in order to emphasise human action; when he is attached to the philosophical idea of providence, instead of proclaiming the supernatural order; when he rationalises about the Church as a human institution; when he rules on facts, on ideas and on men in a way other than that in which the Church rules on them. The author likes to be progressive, to pass for being a man of his time; in a word, he is in too great a rush to receive the acclaim reserved for whomever knows how to be a *man of progress*.

The story of the ancient world is treated according to the naturalist genre when the narrator, instead of showing the imperfection of pagan virtues, accords them an admiration to which they have no right. By pagan virtues I mean here those brilliant qualities and actions whose principle was to realise, not the divine law, but pride, hardness of heart, stoic contempt for life, and the barbarian cult of a material nationality. We know the fateful excitement which this apotheosis of pagan virtues produced at the end of the eighteenth century, and the rage with which the examples of Greece and Rome inspired the monsters of that time. But there is another pitfall that the Christian historian must diligently avoid. As a disciple of revelation, let him take care not to imagine that the gentiles were powerless to come to the knowledge of the true God and, in a sufficient degree, to the realisation of the virtues which honour Him and which are the salvation of man. Supernatural providence, as a means of operating this great design, is one of the objects of Christian history; and, besides the Judaic Church, Catholic theology reveals to us the Church of the gentiles:

less visible, less latent, but still accessible to grace, which has never been totally refused to the human creature, even the most abandoned.

It is not a question here of philosophy, the instrument of pride and deception, but of the Word of God transmitted in an oral manner, fighting against the ever-rising tide of polytheism and rekindled by the succour of that supernatural providence, mentioned earlier, and by a thousand exterior incidents, by a thousand interior touches, which the infinite goodness of God did not reserve only for Christians. Let the Catholic historian never forget this word: "God wills all men to be saved and to come to the knowledge of the truth"; and let him endeavour to discover how, in the ancient world, the entire city of Nineveh knew how to curb the anger of the true God, at the simple word of Jonah; how the centurion, Cornelius, became ready for baptism, even before he knew of the mission of the Saviour. The role of the Jewish people, the resounding prodigies done in their favour, their relations, so extensive at certain periods; their migrations, first to Egypt, then to Assyria, Persia, and even India; the translation of their sacred books into the Greek language in the age of the Ptolemies; their synagogues, spread beyond the limits of the known world and flourishing in the heart of Rome and Greece for centuries before the Man-God appeared; all these facts are so many elements which, even today, make it easy to follow the trail of the supernatural in the annals of the ancient world.

We could mention the oracles, prophets of the gentiles, of whom Scripture gives us the type in Balaam; we could speak of the Sybils, even limiting ourselves to what Cicero and Virgil teach us. Fontenelle was one of the precursors of naturalism in France, and he was not afraid, in an age in which faith still reigned, to brutally deny the most solemn memorials of primitive Christianity, by maintaining that the oracles had not ceased at the coming of Christ; given, he said, that oracles have never been more than a hoax of paganism. It was easy for Christian knowledge to demonstrate that Fontenelle's thesis led to historical Pyrrhonism, and to avenge the good sense of the people of antiquity, gratuitously calumniated by a man already plagued with antipathy to the supernatural.

On his way, the Christian historian of the ancient world will often meet the diabolical supernatural, whose empire had not yet felt the victorious strength of the Cross. Let him not be afraid to depict the harsh slavery of Satan, which weighed upon our gentile fathers over the centuries before the accomplishment of the promise. No man has ever been the proper domain of the spirit of darkness without having merited it; but, in those days, the power of the spirit of lies was much more extensive than it has been since the victory of the Son of God; to deny this explanation of the dreadful disorders of the ancient world would be, for a Christian, not only a culpable act of human respect, but a lack of faith that nothing can justify. Jesus Christ did not disdain to refer to the Devil by his title; He calls him the Prince of this World; and one would think that certain Christian authors of our day have a tendency to take no notice of the numerous passages of the gospel where this perverse dealer is denounced to us as the author of all our ills. They speak of evil, of the spirit of evil, of disorder, of error, of human depravation;

but all this metaphysical language poorly disguises their repugnance for portraying the evil being, who knows how to profit so cleverly from the oversight that he has spread in our days, even as to his very existence. Let it be permitted to say therefore that a history of the ancient world in which one never mentions the name of the eternal enemy of God and man, in which one obstinately tries to explain evil by the sole effect of human perversity and the passions, is neither a Christian history nor a complete history. It has omitted the principal cause of the disorders that it had to account for.

As to the fact of the succession of empires, of the unification of peoples who ought to have been their continuation, of the prophecies that had foretold everything; it is clear that the historian who does not know (or does not want to say) what the goal of all these vicissitudes is, who does not point out the reign of Christ, approaching ever closer with each revolution of the peoples, is blind; and working to keep the rest of the blind in the darkness where he himself is pleased to live. This is history without a goal, in the manner of the pagans who were ignorant of where God was leading the world. Historians see well enough that everything leads to the Roman empire; to this colossal empire which must yield in its turn; but they do not speak of the empire of Jesus Christ, to which the Roman empire had to serve as a stepping-stone. Does Jesus Christ, in their eyes, have an empire? Jesus Christ is the great civiliser of the human race, the one to whom the world owes everything; but to say that He reigns, that He has an empire, that this world is His property, that from now on no one commands here except in His name: this they never dream of doing! *Jesus*

Christ reigns over the minds and morals of man: His kingdom is not in this world. One would think that this really is the thought of many historians, even Christian historians, when one sees them pass over the history of ancient peoples without seeming to suspect that they prepare the way for the Word Incarnate. They say that the coming of Christ is the greatest event of all time, that Christ is the author of the vastest and most salutary regime-change ever accomplished on the globe, but they never allow it to be imagined (and still less do they say) that the earth awaited its king for thousands of years, and that, for nineteen centuries, it has possessed Him.

When our fathers, whose education had been so strongly impregnated with Christianity, enlisted to fight the school of Voltaire — who had dared to claim that Jesus Christ had made humanity worse and that His religion led men to barbarism — it then became necessary to maintain against the philosophers this new, easily demonstrated thesis: that modern civilisation is, in all which is useful to man and society, the daughter of Christianity, and that the pagan religions, polytheism and philosophy led peoples to stupefaction and destruction. At that time, there was no risk in this incontestable point of view, because those who maintained it were not ignorant that Jesus Christ's mission had still other interests, much more precious to man and to society than those which relate to political economy. They knew that the fruits of Christianity, which, even in this present life, place nations which are Christian so far above those which are not, are the pure and simple consequences of other benefits, of an order infinitely superior, which Jesus Christ came to bring us. They knew the gospel by heart; they did not read it in order to look for the verses which they thought could be twisted into the sense of the ideas of the day, while passing over the others in silence. They accepted everything, and they knew perfectly well that, though Jesus Christ announced that the Prince of this World would be cast out, that the redeeming blood would be poured out for the forgiveness of sins, that the human race would be called to form just one flock under the leadership of the Good Shepherd who gives His life for His sheep; this was to say nothing of the political regeneration of the peoples, the civilisation to come, the future conquests of understanding, the progress of the arts and sciences: all advantages which have come to us through Christianity and which would not have come without it. In the entire gospel, there is only one word of Christ's referring to these temporal goods: "Seek ye first the kingdom of God and his justice, and all the rest shall be added unto you." The rest, *caetera*: see how Christ speaks of it, lest we make it the main or even a comparable thing. The defenders of Christianity in the eighteenth century knew and understood all of this, and if they focused on demonstrating the exterior benefits of Christianity (which Julian the Apostate had begun to realise in the fourth century, and for which Turkey envies us today without ever being able to attain them), it was not because they ceased to attach the primary importance to the supernatural benefits, of which the divine mystery of the Incarnation was the source.

Since then, time has passed; modern society, of which some among us are so proud, has begun its somewhat stormy course; Christianity no longer plays a role in public works; legislation does not recognise it as a social bond; and if it is assured of a more or less extensive protection, according to the times, this is not at all because the law recognises it as divine, but uniquely because this cult is supposed to represent the religious interest of the majority. In such a situation, the faith still lives in a great number of souls, so that the fruits of Christianity continue to be produced in a certain measure; but what is the bond of Christians among themselves? How can they unite to form that invincible force which triumphs over paganism? It is, without doubt, by the strength and consistency of the Christian idea; this is where the need is and not elsewhere. One asks, is there any trace of political economy, of utopias, of human perfectibility in the writings of the Christian authors of the first three centuries? And yet, by the fourth century, Christians had become the majority; and Constantine, upon receiving baptism, was just one more Christian. If he had not made himself one, his successor would have been wiser and more clearsighted. How was the conquest carried out? By faith in Jesus Christ crucified, bringing to the world mysteries to believe and supernatural virtues to practise. To the eyes of the first Christians, the era of Christ was not the era of civilisation; they were surrounded with too many crimes and abasements for such an illusion to be possible; for them, the era of Christ was the era of salvation offered to each man, on condition of putting the goods of the life to come, the path to which had just been opened by the Redeemer, before those of the present life. Nothing more and nothing less was necessary to regenerate the world; nothing more and nothing less will be necessary to save it in our own day.

It is therefore a poor tactic for a Christian author who is writing history to present the coming of Christ as the great social revelation and to engage in more or less reinvigorated platitudes on this subject. No one, or almost no one, will contest either your facts or your conclusions, if only you excel in speaking the language of the day. When, then, will it please you to employ your talent to write for Christians? Do you not see that all of these ideas, reproduced with a variety that is only apparent, have the effect of taking men, little by little, away from the supernatural order, whose preponderance in us we maintain only by the effort of faith? Men have more need of someone to repeat to them that Jesus Christ came to redeem them than of someone to say that the object of His mission was to civilise them.

But, you will say, *is it therefore necessary to stop insisting on the consequences of the gospel?* God forbid. All truth is useful, but all truth must be classed according to its importance. Once again, who today dares doubt that Christianity has improved present conditions of life? A few insane and ungodly people whom one does not engage in conversation. The philosophers, the politicians, the smart economists are with you; it is useless, therefore, to launch into the same praise for the great civiliser of modern times. What is urgent, what is to the purpose is to think of the Christians who need to be supported and rallied. And you will only do this by announcing in a loud voice that, under the reign of Augustus Caesar, the only Son of God deigned to take flesh in the womb of a Virgin and to offer Himself in sacrifice to redeem the world of its sins and to break the yoke of Satan who held man enslaved. In speaking thus, you will speak like Saint Augustine and like Bossuet; this may well look a bit like catechism, but do not worry; it is precisely the catechism which is wanting today. The catechism was the basis for the two great historical works of Saint Augustine and Bossuet, and no one says that their talent was any the less for it. Now, if you have something to add to the applications of the gospel for the well-being of man and society, do not deprive yourself of the opportunity. We will listen to you and we will profit by it. Truly, nothing will astonish us, for we are counting on "the rest" — *caetera* — promised by Jesus Christ Himself. All that is needed is that this *caetera* not be the only good that you dare point out in the coming of Christ. We are weak in our faith, our education has often been not quite Christian, the society which surrounds us does not reflect our beliefs; and, to our greater peril, we live at the heart of a social revolution that ferments all kinds of pride.

They might say that writing thus is only a way for you to stock the shelves of parish libraries and reading rooms with your books. Indeed, instead of opening the doors of the Academy to you, perhaps your books, christianly conceived and written, will have the chance to join the *Discourse on Universal History* in these humble repositories; but what misfortune do you see in that? The first necessity today is to fortify and protect Christians in their faith; the second is to increase their number. If you achieve the first goal, you will not have wasted your time. As for the second, you will obviously advance it very little by persuading those who do not believe that those who *do* believe think and speak like them. Besides, we have Catholic writers — a small number, I agree — who, while seeking only pure orthodoxy, have found favour both with simple believers and with people of intelligence and good taste.

And, do you not feel the need to tell the truth, once and for all, to your contemporaries? Have we not flattered and misled them long enough by upholding the truth only up to a point, colouring over that which is most ancient and most immutable with a dubious, modern varnish? You are correct; we have discovered who-knows-what neutral ground on which certain believers meet with unbelievers to hold a kind of congress, from which everyone leaves in the same state as he arrived; but what results from these rapprochements? Mutual compliments and, while waiting for something else to come of it: *society*, which is perishing because no one speaks frankly to it of Jesus Christ; because no one requires you to account for your talents, for your influence, for your Christian convictions even, so often disguised under your naturalist exterior? It is time to imbue your words with a more Christian accent, and to write books in a tone which would be well placed in the heart of the family. You would not instruct your children in their religion using naturalistic theories; you would be afraid of not making them Christians. You teach them the catechism; would that you would teach it to them also by your example; would that your books, speeches and public writings were likewise the expression of it. The moment is all the more opportune if you notice the good will with which you are heard. Take a step and, from now on, recount the facts of history in the tone of a convinced Christian, who feels the need to proclaim that all progress is in Jesus Christ and through Jesus Christ. You will then be a worthy historian before God and men.

It is known from experience that the men of today who are not believers fail to guess anything for themselves as regards principles in religious matters. This powerlessness results from too cautious a silence that we have kept towards them for too long and which permits them to remain completely ignorant. It is impossible not to be struck by the dedication and quiet heroism of the Sisters of Charity. Most likely, one is generally able to account for the determining principle of this dedication and heroism: one knows that *religious sense* is the source. But what idea can those who do not have the light of faith, among the people who ask for their help, form of the religious sense which animates these Sisters? Because, after all, religious sense is found everywhere that a religion exists. Why is it that such dedication did not exist among the ancient religions of the world? Why is it that, among the Christian peoples, one only encounters it in those who are of the Roman communion? It must therefore be the fruit of a particular dogma which is not found elsewhere. They should have examined this point, in this age where they love to account for everything, where they generate statistics about everything. They have not done it. While approving of the work, they limit themselves to wondering. In fact, it is quite simple; it is only a matter of telling those who are interested: You have the Sisters of Charity serving you, because a priesthood exists, founded by Jesus Christ, and the members of this priesthood exercise the power to purify souls and bring them into contact with God Himself, in a mystery that we call Communion, of which they are the ministers. If this priesthood would cease to act, if it were driven out of our society, you would see the race of these servants of the poor and the sick extinguished in the same blow. That which you call religious sense could not produce them anymore, still less multiply them.

Thus, a question of revealed dogma is naturally introduced to resolve the particular problem of which we are speaking; it is no doubt the same for all the other questions which can be raised on the diverse forms of progress enjoyed by Christian nations. Our fathers, who were Christian by tradition, were not ignorant of it when they discussed the question of Christian economics with the philosophers of their time; but we no longer know it, and this is why it is necessary that we be told it, at the risk of scaring some away. And yet it is proper, in historical accounts, to know how to put into words everything which is important to know. What is the good of an historical account which describes the effects without frankly admitting the causes? It has been said and it bears repeating: the destiny of the human race is a supernatural destiny. It follows from this that a history which does not draw its inspiration from supernatural sources is not a true history, however Christian the convictions of the author may be in other respects.

www.ingramcontent.com/pod-product-compliance
Lightning Source LLC
Chambersburg PA
CBHW060505080526
44584CB00015B/1558

9781838478520